Little Teddy helps Mouse

Story by Beverley Randell
Illustrations by Chantal Stewart

Mouse said,

"Little Teddy! Little Teddy!

Where are you going?"

"I am going to the store,"
said Little Teddy.

"Can I come too?"
said Mouse.

"Can I come to the store?"

"Mouse! Mouse!"

shouted Little Teddy.

"Look down!

Look at the big puddle!"

Mouse went into the puddle.

"Oh! Oh!" he said.

"Where am I?" said Mouse.

"You are in the big puddle," said Little Teddy.

Mouse said, "Look at me!"

"Come on, Mouse," said Little Teddy.

"Come here."

Little Teddy and Mouse went home.

"Thank you, Little Teddy,"

said Mouse.